S0-ASN-916

For

ANGELS
In Our Midst

Edited by Liesl Vazquez
Design by Deborah Michel

PETER PAUPER PRESS, INC
WHITE PLAINS . NEW YORK

With love to Steve, and
special thanks to S. S. Z.

Peter Pauper Press, Inc.
202 Mamaroneck Avenue
White Plains, NY 10601

ISBN 0-88088-946-2
Printed in Singapore
7 6 5 4 3 2 1

Angel image on the jacket is
from the private collection of
Diane and Ralph Hellebuyck, Sr.
Reprinted with permission.

Introduction

Throughout the ages, angels have graced our lives as symbols of love, kindness, mercy and, most especially, as messengers between Earth and the Heavens. The influence of angels reaches far and wide, for they embody the highest ideals to which we all aspire.

Whether real or imaginary, angels are so beloved that they have been adopted as part of our year-round and holiday lore. Although angels first appeared as religious beings, their influence has spread to secular fields as well.

Angels now adorn our everyday world, lifting our spirits and warming our hearts.

This Keepsake offers a glimpse into the glorious and varied realms in which angels gather. *Angels in Our Midst* explores your own angelic self, the religious origins and prevalence of angels, angels and love, guardian angels, angels and food, and angels in literature, film, and music. Each chapter, which combines prose and witty quotes, is sure to evoke the angel in you.

So, turn the page and indulge your flights of fancy. And remember, as G. K. Chesterton said, *Angels can fly because they take themselves lightly.*

L. V.

Contents

The Angel within You

For every angel fluttering through the skies, there is a divine counterpart here on Earth. Each of us has a golden celestial self just waiting to be awakened. Allow the angel within you to emerge in expressions of loving thoughts and kindnesses. Let us always truly be *on the side of the angels*.

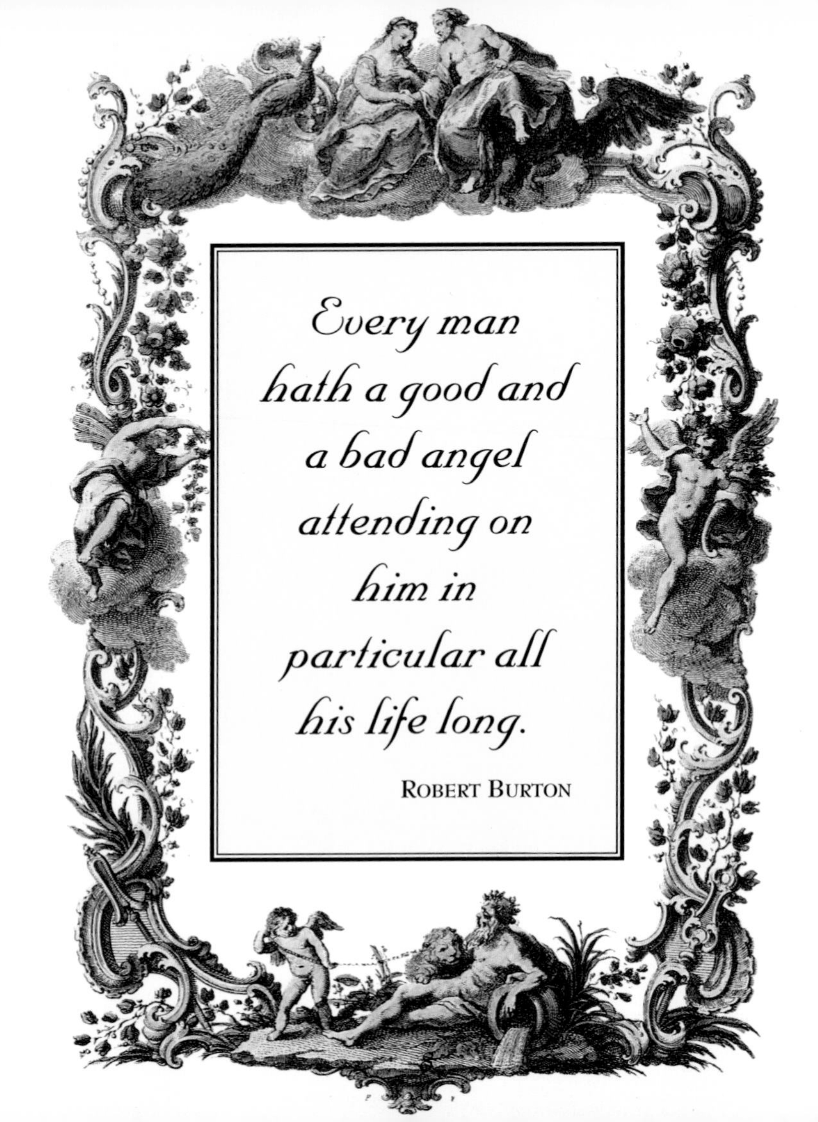

Every man
hath a good and
a bad angel
attending on
him in
particular all
his life long.

ROBERT BURTON

If I see one dilemma with Western man, it's that he can't accept how beautiful he is. He can't accept that he is pure light, that he's pure love, that he's pure consciousness, that he's divine.

RAM DASS (RICHARD ALPERT)

The devil could change. He was once an angel and may be evolving still.

LAURENCE J. PETER

If a man is not rising upward to be an angel, depend upon it, he is sinking downward to be a devil.

SAMUEL TAYLOR COLERIDGE

Men prefer to believe that they are degenerated angels, rather than elevated apes.

W. WINWOOD ROADE

If God could make angels, why did he bother with men?

DAGOBERT D. RUNES

The question is this: Is man an ape or an angel? Now, I am on the side of the angels.

BENJAMIN DISRAELI

Time is man's angel.

JOHANN VON SCHILLER

Everyone entrusted with a mission is an angel... All forces that reside in the body are angels.

MOSES MAIMONIDES

Historical and Religious Origins of Angels

The religious or historical origins of angels trace back to the Bible, where angels served as messengers from God. Later, both Dionysius in *Celestial Hierarchy* and Thomas Aquinas in *Summa Theologica* categorized angels into a hierarchical structure:

RANK	ANGELS	CHARACTERISTICS
First Order	*Seraphim, cherubim, thrones*	*Purity, knowledge, God's messengers*
Second Order	*Dominations, virtues, powers*	*Patience, courage, governors of the soul*
Third Order	*Principalities, archangels, angels*	*Defenders of religion, human-like qualities*

And again, when he bringeth in the first begotten into the world, he saith, And let all all the angels of God worship him.

HEBREWS (KJV)

In all their affliction he was afflicted, and the angel of his presence saved them: in his love and in his pity he redeemed them; and he bare them, and carried them all the days of old.

ISAIAH 63:9 (KJV)

Suffer not thy mouth to cause thy flesh to sin; neither say thou before the angel, that it was an error: wherefore should God be angry at thy voice, and destroy the work of thine hands?

ECCLESIASTES 5:6 (KJV)

And there appeared an angel unto him from heaven, strengthening him.

LUKE 22:43 (KJV)

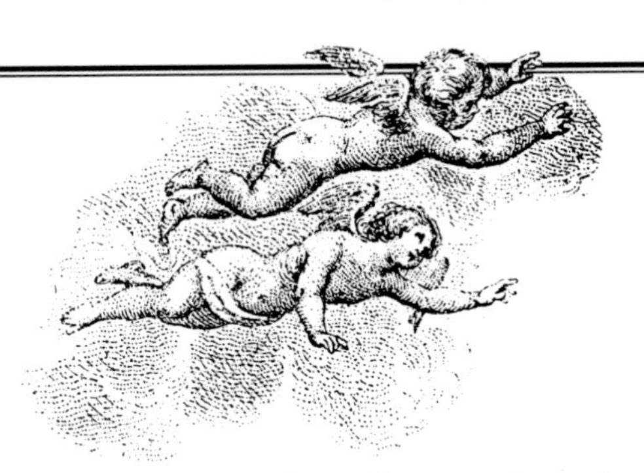

And no marvel; for Satan himself is transformed into an angel of light.

II CORINTHIANS 11:14 (KJV)

Know ye not that we shall judge angels? how much more things that pertain to this life?

I CORINTHIANS 6:3 (KJV)

For when they shall rise from the dead, they neither marry, nor are given in marriage; but are as the angels which are in heaven.

MARK 12:25 (KJV)

For an angel went down at a certain season into the pool, and troubled the water: whosoever then first after the troubling of the water stepped in was made whole of whatsoever disease he had.

JOHN 5:4 (KJV)

The angel Gabriel was sent from God unto a city of Galilee, named Nazareth,

To a virgin espoused to a man whose name was Joseph, of the house of David; and the virgin's name was Mary.

And the angel came in unto her, and said, Hail, thou that art highly favored, the Lord is with thee: blessed art thou among women.

LUKE 1:26-28 (KJV)

Angels in Different Religions

Angels are featured in Christianity, Judaism, Islam, and other religions. In countless Old and New Testament verses, we find angels performing their chief function—acting as God's messengers. Other religions, including Buddhism and Hinduism, mention angels throughout their scriptures as well. Read the following passages and gain a greater understanding of how angels are depicted.

When Adam was in the Garden of Eden, he used to recline while the ministering angels roasted flesh and filtered wine for him.

Mishnah

When a man dies they who survive him ask what property he has left behind. The angel who bends over the dying man asks what good deeds he has sent before him.

The Koran

I believe we are free, within limits, and yet there is an unseen hand, a guiding angel, that somehow, like a submerged propeller, drives us on.

Rabindranath Tagore

Every visible thing in this world is put in the charge of an angel.

St. Augustine

A demon holds a book, in which are written the sins of a particular man; an Angel drops on it from a phial, a tear which the sinner had shed in doing a good action, and his sins are washed out.

ALBERIC, MONK OF MONTE-CASSINO

Praise be to Allah, the creator of the heavens and earth, who maketh the angels his messengers, and giveth them two, three or four pairs of wings.

THE KORAN

The angel of the Lord encampeth round about them that fear him, and delivereth them.

PSALMS 34:7 (KJV)

The enemy that sowed them is the devil; the harvest is the end of the world; and the reapers are the angels.

MATTHEW 13:39 (KJV)

Guardian Angels

While all angels are beings of sublime goodness, guardian angels serve especially as protectors and caretakers of individuals here on earth. You may not recognize or acknowledge your guardian angel, but he or she watches, guides, and defends you at all times. Your guardian angel also soothes and pacifies you, and gives you peace of mind in times of crisis. Let your guardian angel's good will enfold you throughout and beyond the holiday season!

It is a universal Catholic belief that not merely every *just* man, every child of grace, but in fact *every single human being* here upon earth, whether Christian or non-Christian, whether in grace or sin, remains during its entire life under the care of a Guardian Angel.

JOSEPH HUSSLEIN

The guardian angels of life sometimes fly so high as to be beyond our sight, but they are always looking down upon us.

JEAN PAUL RICHTER

Make yourself familiar with the angels, and behold them frequently in spirit; for, without being seen, they are present with you.

ST. FRANCIS OF SALES

We should pray to the angels, for they are given to us as guardians.

ST. AMBROSE

We not only live among men, but there are airy hosts, blessed spectators, sympathetic lookers-on, that see and know and appreciate our thoughts and feelings and acts.

HENRY WARD BEECHER

Each of us has a guardian angel. They're nonthreatening, wise and loving beings. They offer help whether we ask for it or not. But mostly we ignore them.

EILEEN FREEMAN

At dusk three angels come down from the sky to every house. One stands at the door, another sits at the table, and a third watches over the bed. They look after the house and protect it. Neither wolves nor evil spirits can enter the whole night long.

CARLO LEVI

Therefore for spirits, I am so far from denying their existence that I could easily believe that not only whole Countries, but particular persons, have their Tutelary and Guardian Angels.

THOMAS BROWNE

Angels and Love

Along with flowers and hearts, soaring angels have become symbols of love and romance. Cherubs—*love angels* depicted as chubby, winged babies—were originally multi-bodied beasts, but how they were transformed remains unknown. Cupid, a popular Valentine's cherub, is always portrayed with a bow and arrow. Couples fall in love when pierced by one of his magical arrows. Delight in the dreamy quotes that follow, and surrender yourself to Cupid's charms.

We are each of us angels with only one wing. And we can only fly embracing each other.

LUCIANO DE CRESCENZO

Immortal Cherubims! And young men glittering and sparkling angels, and maids strange seraphic pieces of life and beauty! Boys and girls tumbling in the street, and playing, were moving jewels.

THOMAS TRAHERNE

She is as pure, as good, and as beautiful as an angel.

GUY DE MAUPASSANT

Love is how you earn your wings.

KAREN GOLDMAN

The power to love what is purely abstract is given to few.

MARGOT ASQUITH

Thou hast the sweetest face I ever looked on;
Sir, as I have a soul, she is an angel.

SHAKESPEARE AND JOHN FLETCHER,
HENRY VIII

Angels and archangels may have gathered there,
Cherubim and seraphim thronged the air;
But his mother only, in her maiden bliss,
Worshipped the beloved with a kiss.

CHRISTINA ROSSETTI

'Tis strange what a man may do, and a woman yet think him an angel.

WILLIAM MAKEPEACE THACKERAY

Literary Angels

Just as angels abound in different religions and religious texts, they also flourish in the world's great secular prose and poetry. Transcend the ordinary and indulge in these verses from Keats, Voltaire, Chekhov, and a heavenly host of other renowned writers.

We shall find peace. We shall hear the angels, we shall see the sky sparkling with diamonds.

ANTON CHEKHOV

All the Utopias will come to pass only when we grow wings and all people are converted into angels.

FËDOR DOSTOEVSKI

It is not known precisely where angels dwell—whether in the air, the void, or the planets. It has not been God's pleasure that we should be informed of their abode.

VOLTAIRE

Then cherish pity, lest you drive an angel from your door.

WILLIAM BLAKE

It is in rugged crises, in unweariable endurance, and in aims which put sympathy out of the question, that the angel is shown.

RALPH WALDO EMERSON

Millions of spiritual creatures walk the earth unseen, both when we sleep and when we wake.

JOHN MILTON

Philosophy will clip an angel's wings.

JOHN KEATS

The angels laughed.

God looked down from his seventh heaven and smiled.

The angels spread their wings and, together with Elijah, flew upward into the sky.

ISAAC BASHEVIS SINGER

Angels in Music

Angels, because of their inherent goodness and divinity, are ideal topics for songs. Their association with beauty and benevolence is seen in song titles such as *Earth Angel* and *Angel Of The Morning*. Included here are the lyrics to some well-loved *angelic* Christmas songs.

Hark! The Herald Angels Sing

Hark! the herald angels sing,
Glory to the newborn King;
Peace on earth, and mercy mild,
God and sinners reconciled!
Joyful, all ye nations, rise,
Join the triumph of the skies;
With th'angelic hosts proclaim,
Christ is born in Bethlehem!

Refrain
Hark! the herald angels sing,
Glory to the newborn King.

Christ, by highest heaven adored;
Christ, the everlasting Lord;
Late in time behold Him come,
Offspring of the virgin's womb.
Veiled in flesh the Godhead see;
Hail th'Incarnate Deity,

Pleased as man with man to dwell;
Jesus, our Emmanuel.

Refrain
Hail, the heav'n born Prince of Peace!
Hail, the Sun of Righteousness!

Music is well said to be the speech of angels.

THOMAS CARLYLE

Angels dance in step to their own rhythms in harmony with the greatest and smallest rhythms of the universe.

KAREN GOLDMAN

And flights of angels sing thee to thy rest!

WILLIAM SHAKESPEARE, *HAMLET*

Angels We Have Heard on High

Angels we have heard on high,
Sweetly singing o'er the plains,
And the mountains in reply,
Echoing their joyous strains.
Gloria in excelsis Deo,
Gloria in excelsis Deo.

Shepherds, why this jubilee?
Why your joyous songs prolong?
What the gladsome tidings be
Which inspire your heav'nly song?
Gloria in excelsis Deo,
Gloria in excelsis Deo.

Come to Bethlehem and see
Him whose birth the angels sing;
Come, adore on bended knee,
Christ the Lord, the newborn King.
Gloria in excelsis Deo,
Gloria in excelsis Deo.

The Angel Gabriel

The Angel Gabriel from God
Was sent to Galilee,
Unto a virgin fair and free,
Whose name was called Mary.
And when the Angel thither came,
He fell down on his knee,
And looking up in the virgin's face,
He said, *All hail, Mary.*

Refrain
Then sing we all, both great and small,
Nowell, Nowell, Nowell;
We may rejoice to hear the voice
Of the Angel Gabriel.

Mary anon looked him upon,
And said, *Sir what are ye?*
I marvel much at these tidings
Which thou hast brought to me.

Married I am unto an old man,
As the lot fell unto me;
Therefore, I pray, depart away,
For I stand in doubt of thee.

Refrain

Whether the angels play only Bach in praising God I am not quite sure; I am sure, however, that en famille they play Mozart.

KARL BARTH

I heard a soft melodious voice, more pure and harmonious than any I had heard with my ears before; I believed it was the voice of an angel who spake to the other angels.

JOHN WOOLMAN

Angels from the Realms of Glory

Angels from the realms of glory,
Wing your flight o'er all the earth.
Ye, who sang creation's story,
Now proclaim Messiah's birth.
Come and worship!
Come and worship!
Worship Christ the new-born King!

Shepherds in the field abiding,
Watching o'er your flocks by night.
God with man is now residing,
Yonder shines the infant Light. *(chorus)*

Sages, leave your contemplations,
Brighter visions beam afar.
Seek the great Desire of nations;
Ye have seen his natal star. *(chorus)*

48

Screen Angels

One might expect angels to appear on the big screen in the form of airy wisps on gossamer wings, but in fact earthly angels are far more prevalent. Time after time, angels have been featured in films, most often in the form of guardian angels who change the course of human lives. Consider Clarence, a wingless angel in Frank Capra's *It's a Wonderful Life*, sent down to Earth to rescue a down-and-out family man (Jimmy Stewart) from taking his own life. Although Stewart's character sees Clarence as a *sort of fallen angel*, Clarence succeeds in his mission, as do all movie angels.

You can't pin sergeant's stripes on an archangel.

Millard Mitchell,
in *A Foreign Affair*

Good night, my angel, my sweet boy.

Joanne Woodward to Tom Hanks,
in *Philadelphia*

Yes, angel, I'm gonna send you over.

Humphrey Bogart to Mary Astor,
in *The Maltese Falcon*

I'm going to find me an angel. I'm going to find me a real hootenanny of an angel. If she gives me any trouble, she's going to find herself with them little old wings just pinned right to the ground.

Don Murray,
in *Bus Stop*

Well, you look about like the kind of angel I'd get. Sort of a fallen angel, aren't you? What happened to your wings?

JIMMY STEWART TO HENRY TRAVERS,
IN *IT'S A WONDERFUL LIFE*

Every time you hear a bell ring, it means that some angel's just got his wings.

HENRY TRAVERS TO JIMMY STEWART,
IN *IT'S A WONDERFUL LIFE*

I've never before had to fight an angel, but I suggest you take off your coat and put up your dukes.

DAVID NIVEN TO CARY GRANT,
IN *THE BISHOP'S WIFE*

Excuse me while I slip into something more comfortable.

JEAN HARLOW,
IN *HELL'S ANGELS*

Angels and Food

With angels involved in so many facets of our lives, it's no wonder we find them invading even the foods we eat! You may begin with an entree of angel hair pasta and top it off with a slice of angel food cake for dessert, but whether you follow one of these recipes or create your own menu, be sure to savor these angelic treats.

Angel Hair Pasta with Heavenly Shellfish

2 cans (14-1/2 oz. each) stewed tomatoes
1 can (16 oz.) tomato sauce
2 large cloves garlic, crushed
1-1/2 teaspoons Italian seasoning
1 teaspoon sugar
Salt and freshly ground pepper to taste
1 pound shrimp, shelled and deveined
2 dozen mussels, scrubbed
2 dozen Little Neck clams, rinsed
1 pound angel hair pasta, cooked and drained
Freshly grated Parmesan cheese to serve
Freshly chopped parsley to garnish

Place stewed tomatoes, tomato sauce, garlic, Italian seasoning, sugar, salt, and pepper in large saucepan. Stir well, bring to a boil, reduce heat, and simmer 5 minutes. Add shrimp, mussels, and clams. Cover and simmer just until mussels and clams open. Discard any that don't open. Place cooked angel hair in large serving bowl. Spoon sauce and shellfish over and toss gently. Sprinkle with Parmesan cheese and garnish with parsley. Serve immediately.

6 servings

Angels are sweet and sour and salty, wet and dry, hard and soft, sharp and smooth. They fly, yes, but in flights of our own fancy.

F. FORRESTER CHURCH

Man did eat angels' food: he sent them meat to the full.

PSALMS 78:25 (KJV)

Angel Food Cake

1 cup sifted cake flour
1-1/4 cups sugar, divided
10 egg whites
1 teaspoon cream of tartar
1/4 teaspoon salt
1 teaspoon vanilla extract
1/4 teaspoon almond extract

Preheat oven at 350°. Sift flour 3 times with 1/2 cup sugar. Beat egg whites until foamy. Add cream of tartar and salt and beat until stiff but not dry. Whip in remaining sugar, 2 tablespoons at a time. Add vanilla and almond extract. Sift about 1/4 cup of flour and sugar mixture at a time over the batter and fold in until no flour shows. Turn into an ungreased 10-inch tube pan and bake for 45 minutes. Invert pan on neck of a bottle or funnel and let cake cool thoroughly in pan.